# CAN I PAY MYSELF?

## A HOW-TO BUDGETING GUIDE FOR ENTREPRENEURS

Authored by:

Jeremy Knight, DVM

The Barklee Institute
1001 E FM 700
Big Spring, TX 79720
www.thebarkleeinstitute.com



Interior Layout: The Book Makers; Tracy Atkins
Cover Design: The Book Makers; Tanja Prokop
Illustrator: Chelsea Lybeck
Initial Editor: Mike Lewis
Copyeditor: The Book Makers; Sarah Brown

Can I Pay Myself? / Jeremy Knight, DVM. -- 1st ed.

Print ISBN: 978-0-578-83691-1
eBook ISBN: 978-0-578-83693-5

barklee
be money savvy

# CONTENTS

# INTRODUCTION: CONVINCE ME I NEED A BUDGET

My wife and I were 5 months into starting our own business when we realized we did not have a clue where our money was going. We had accepted the reality that our salaries would decrease in the beginning, but the quasi-math I did in my head assured me we would be fine. I did not realize that the realistic version of "doing fine" meant we were 1 month from going broke. So, where was all of our money going?

We wanted to buy a new house like everyone else, but we could not seem to scrape together a down payment. We were starting to realize that our debt payments were quickly overwhelming our monthly income. The simple fact was that if our business did not make enough money, then it would fail to provide for our family. Our family was the whole reason we got into this "entrepreneurial startup" in the first place.

We were quickly becoming a statistic, and we were going to fail with our small business just like the 80% of startups that had failed before us. We were no different, our excuses were no different, and our lack of financial reporting or budgeting was no different than the failures before us. Did you know that the #1 cause for small business failure within 2.5 to 5 years is due to cash flow issues? I am sure Instagram has taught you that already, but what does it mean? Simply put, it means that the business ran out of money.

I am putting effort into this book for one reason—so that your entrepreneurial startup does not fail to provide for your family. And the best place to start is with the #1 cause of small business failure—budgeting and cash flow. Budgeting gives you the safety of spending only what is available this month so that you can live to fight another month. It shows you where frivolous spending is occurring so that you can cut it out and put that money towards the pieces of your business that create profit. In a nutshell, the budget is the one piece of information that will help you identify cash flow problems before they cause you to fail.

In the following pages, I'll explain the importance of creating a budget for your home and your home-based business, the differences between a home and business budget, and how to combine business and home budgets for a true picture of how you are affected by your new business. Finally, I will include examples of budgets for a household and a home-based business so that you can create your own immediately after reading this book. Remember, money management is not hard; it is just a skill that takes knowledge and practice.

# CHAPTER 1.
# WHAT IS A BUDGET?

The word "budget" refers to a **recorded list of estimated income and expenses for a future period.** It is rooted in the fifteenth-century French word *"bouge,"* meaning "leather bag, wallet, pouch." Some believe its use in modern finance comes from the practice of treasury ministers keeping their financial plans in a wallet or bag.[1] Budgets and the practice of budgeting have been used by individuals and organizations for hundreds of years, at least as long as currency has existed.

## HOW DO BUDGETS DIFFER FROM OTHER FINANCIAL REPORTS?

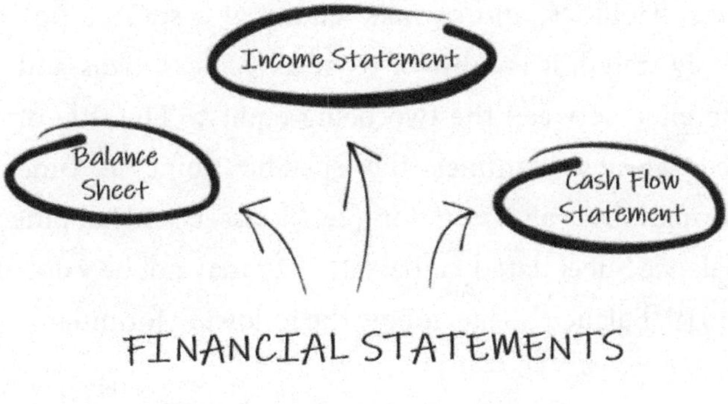


[1] Online Etymology Dictionary website. (Accessed June 11, 2020) https://www.etymonline.com/word/budget

Many entrepreneurs confuse a budget with other reports used to communicate information about past results or the current financial state of a business. While there are similarities between the different reports, their purposes vary. The most common financial statements are used to capture and display financial information for past periods. They are typically reviewed simultaneously for an accurate analysis of a business.

They include the following:

- **Income Statement**. Also known as the profit and loss statement, this report details the revenues and expenses of a company over a specific past period. An annual income statement, for example, provides information for one year of operation. A monthly income statement would show similar information for a single month. An income statement focuses on income and costs within the defined period using the following formula:

  *Total Revenues – Total Costs = Profits.*

- An income statement always includes the beginning and ending dates of the period covered in its title (i.e., Income Statement for period January 1, 2019 to December 31, 2019).
- **Balance Sheet**. This financial statement reports a company's assets, liabilities, and owners' equity at a specific point in time. Simply stated, it is a list of what a business owns and owes, the difference between the two being equity. The title of a Balance Sheet always identifies the specific point in time that the information is valid. For example, the assets and liabilities listed on a Balance Sheet dated January 1, 2019 may not be valid on January 2, 2019. Balance Sheets follow the following formula:

  *Assets = Liabilities + Owners' Equity.*

- **Cash Flow Statement**. Sometimes called a Sources and Uses Statement, this report details the cash flowing into a business from all sources and the cash flowing out of the business for any reason over a specific period. Cash flow statements typically apply to the same period as an accompanying Income Statement but do not consider profit and loss during the period.

A Budget is also a financial report that appears most like the Income Statement or the Cash Flow Statement with a major difference. An income statement, balance sheet, and cash flow statement always reflect the past while a budget is an estimate of revenues and expenses for a future defined period. The three reports help managers understand what happened in the past, but they are powerless to change the results. **A budget forecasts the future, allowing managers to make operational changes to change the results.**

## WHY BUDGET?

Using a budget in a home-based business benefits an entrepreneur by emphasizing:

- **Financial control.** A budget requires estimating the level of future income and expenses to ensure the business can pay its ongoing expenses and fund future projects when needed. Just as a government should not go to war without knowing that future tax collections will be available to pay the projected costs of maintaining their army, small business owners should not contract for future supplies or make long-term investments without a realistic view of their future income.
- **Prioritization of objectives.** Most people learn early in life that there is never enough money to acquire all the things we desire. Whether you are a teenager deciding to buy the latest Nike sports shoe or attending the upcoming Taylor Swift concert to the businessperson torn between hiring a new employee or initiating a new social media marketing campaign, everyone makes choices. A household budget helps families live within their means and

prepare for the future. A business budget graphically displays the financial capacity of a business to continue to operate, grow, or retrench without change.

- **Financial goal-setting**. Budgets translate vague mission statements and ambiguous goals into specific, tangible financial objectives that can be measured and documented. If I tell you that I am going to Florida in the summer, what images come to mind? Compare those thoughts to the images that occur if I say, "I am going to Disneyworld on July 4th." The contrast of my statements is like working with and without a budget.
- **Performance measurement**. The individual line items of a budget function simultaneously as goals and restraints. Success or failure is not subjective but objective. The result is a simple pass or fail when financial results are compared to the budget.
- **Management by exception**. About sixty percent of home-based businesses have one employee, the founding entrepreneur. [2] Consequently, he or she is the CEO, the Cook, and the Chief Bottle-Washer. Everything that happens in the company is their responsibility even though many still perform household and family duties. There are simply not enough hours in the day to take care of everything that might arise. Operating with a budget is a crucial time-saver. Rather than worry about all aspects of the company, the entrepreneur can focus on exceptions—those areas that are outside of the budget targets.

Every business succeeds or fails by its ability to make a profit (i.e., secure a flow of income greater than the outflow of expenses). The first objective of every business owner is to reach "break-even"—the point in time where income equals expenses.

[2] Frequently asked questions about small business. U.S. Small Business Administration Office of Advocacy website. (Accessed June 12, 2020) https://www.sba.gov/sites/default/files/advocacy/SB-FAQ-2017-WEB.pdf

Some companies never achieve break-even while others take months and even years before that point is reached. When cash flow into a company is less than cash outflow, the gap must be covered by funds from outside of the business in the form of loans or additional investment. The budget is an early warning system that alerts households and businesses of potential dangers ahead. When properly created and maintained, it signals whether future expenditures are possible or probable.

It is my experience that the owner of a home-based business requires a household budget **and** a business budget. In many cases, the home-based business is funded by household income after paying household expenses, at least for a time. Trying to get a new business off the ground without knowing if you will have extra income is like starting a long automobile trip without knowing how much gas is in the car. I will detail the general steps to create a budget for the home or the business, noting crucial differences as you implement the process.

# CHAPTER 2.
# COMMON ISSUES IN CREATING A BUSINESS BUDGET

Some entrepreneurs become mesmerized by the potential of their business idea, certain that customers will rush to buy their new product or service as soon as the doors open. They do not create budgets because they believe break-even and profitability will be achieved quickly after opening. Others delay budgeting until sometime later when the business is up and running, initially focused on the minutiae of creating a business. Some postpone the budgeting task because they are unfamiliar with the process or lack information. Despite their misgivings, opening or operating a business without a budget is akin to walking through a maze blindfolded. The likelihood of success is low.

## LACK OF FAMILIARITY WITH BUSINESS BUDGETS

Eighty percent of American families use a household budget regularly.[3] That is not a surprise since financial experts on television and radio from Dave Ramsey to Suze Orman recommend budgeting for everything from getting out of debt to saving for a college education. At the same time, many home-business owners who are comfortable creating a family budget shy

[3] Debt.com's 2020 budgeting survey reveals ,ore Americans than ever are budgeting. Debt.com website. (Accessed June 12, 2020) https://www.debt.com/research/best-way-to-budget-2019/

away from using a budget in their business. Their reluctance stems from previous experiences with budgets in large companies or fear of obscure accounting terms. After reading my book, you will discover that business budgets are no more difficult to construct and use than a familiar household budget.

## CONCERNS ABOUT ACCURACY

How can I budget my business income if I do not know what I might make? This question arises frequently when I recommend budgeting to a new business owner. The answer is "use your best guess." If you plan to start or have started a business, you have some idea about the sales you expect as well as the rate that the sales volume might grow in the future.

Will your estimates be right? Probably not. Economist Edgar R. Fielder, former Assistant Secretary of The Treasury under Presidents Ford and Nixon, noted, "He who lives by the crystal ball soon learns to eat ground glass."[4] Even so, one of the greatest minds of the twentieth century, mathematician Henri Poincaré, claimed, "It is far better to foresee even without certainty than not to foresee at all."[5] I'll discuss the advantage of using conservative estimates of income and expenses later in the book.

## MINGLING HOUSEHOLD AND BUSINESS EXPENSES

Many home-based business owners co-mingle their personal and business accounts, especially if the business is a sole proprietor or a family

[4] Fielder, E. The three R;s of economic forecasting – irrational, irrelevant, and irreverent. Across the Board. June 1977. Pp.62-63.

[5] Poincaré, H. The Foundations of Science. The Science Press, New York and Garrison, N.Y. 1921. P.129
https://www.google.com/books/edition/The_Foundations_of_Science/WxLJzL4e4wsC?hl=en&gbpv=1&dq=The+Foundations+of+Science&printsec=frontcover

partnership. Consequently, determining what expense is for the household and what expense is for business can be confusing.

> *TIP: Separate the two activities with separate banking, credit, and accounting records. In addition to presenting a more professional image to the public, maintaining separate records facilitates tax filings and reduces the likelihood of a tax audit due to the co-mingling of deductions.*

Consider the case of a self-employed writer who subscribes to multiple digital magazines and newspapers for research, an expense that can easily exceed several thousand dollars each year. The U.S. Internal Revenue Service's (IRS) current rules disallow tax deductions for such expenses unless they are incurred by a business. For tax reasons alone, a home-based business should maintain two separate bank accounts, credit cards, and budgets—one for the household and one for the business—even when the business results will be reported on Schedule C (Profit or Loss from a Business) on the proprietor's Income Tax Form 1040.

Maintaining two budgets—one for the household and one for the business—is only common sense.

# CHAPTER 3.
# BUDGET PLANNING CYCLE

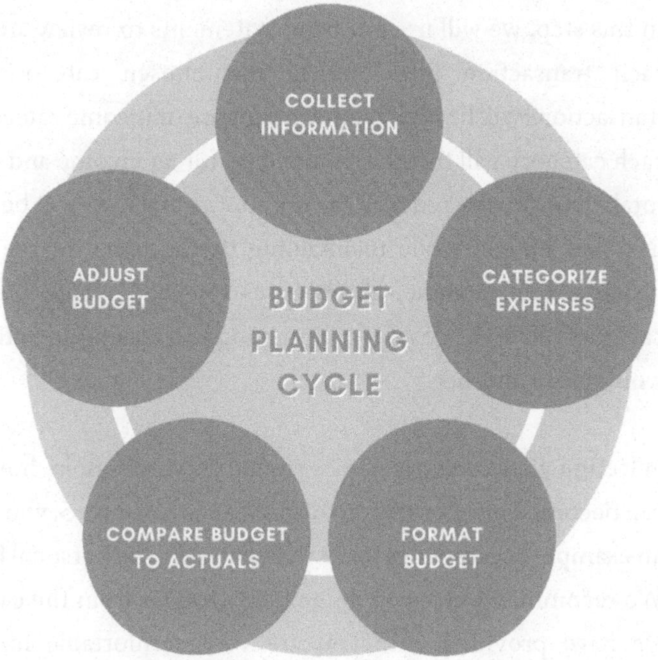


Budgeting is a habit everyone should develop. The budget process consists of several sequential steps, whether creating a household or a home-based business budget. As new information appears, the cycle is repeated over and over to improve the forecasts and make the budget more valuable as a management tool. The five steps in the process are:

1. **Collect information**. The quality of a decision depends on the quality of information available to understand the problem and its possible solution. The initial information needed for a household budget is data about past income and expenses, while the information needed for a business budget is typically industry data and informed estimates. The best place to find your past information with the greatest accuracy is your bank and credit card statements, and we will cover this in detail inside Chapter 4.
2. **Categorize Expenses**. Categories are called "Chart of Accounts" in the accounting profession, and they provide the user with a way to organize and condense the transactions that occur each month. In this step, we will use our bank statements to review and group each transaction into one of our chosen categories. The transactions will be placed into an expense or income category, and each category will then be summed up for an income and expense total. This greatly reduces the amount of data we will be placing into our budget while maintaining the accuracy of the budget formula. For example, all expenses for food would be in one category while the costs of maintaining and driving an automobile would be in another.

   Selecting your category names should be very simple; however, it can become quite complex to beginners. In Chapter 5, you will find an example of categories for both businesses and personal budgets. We recommend that you do not stray too far from the categories we have provided until you are very comfortable in making budgets.

3. **Format Budget**. The fourth step in the process is transferring the categories and their respective sums to a pre-designed budget template or your own custom Excel budget. Documenting the

budget is important because it establishes income and expense targets for a household or business.

4. **Adjust the Zero-Based budget**. Be very clear about the goal of a budget; a budget tells every dollar where it will be spent before you spend it. This means that your budget should always equal zero before you are done. We cannot spend more in a month than we make, and we should never leave our money with no purpose. If your expense totals leave a positive net income, then adjust your debt payments, savings, giving, investments, or recreational spending until the net income is zero.

   Life has a way of throwing surprises at us so we need to remain flexible throughout the month. If you find that you are going to overspend in one category, then go back to the budget and adjust another category for compensation. For example, if you under-budgeted for groceries this month because your child had an unexpected soccer team get together at your house, then decrease the amount you will spend on eating out to make up for it.

5. **Compare budget to actuals**. As each budget period ends, compare actual income and expenditures with the projected budget amounts. Treat the household and business budgets separately. All variances greater than 5% should be analyzed to determine whether they are justified and likely to be continued or temporary.

*TIP: When preparing your budgets for the first time, it is likely that some steps will overlap so that you are executing multiple steps simultaneously. Nevertheless, I have found completing each step before beginning the next is a great time-saver.*

# CHAPTER 4.
# COLLECT INFORMATION

The most common mistake that people make when starting to budget is failing to know their historical spending patterns. When developing a household budget, it is common to make assumptions about expenses based on rules of thumb—such as 10% of income for food—or averages they find on the internet. For example, one source reported that a typical single person spends $660 per month on food, $372 at home, and $228 away from home. In my experience, few people fit the averages.

Developing a home-based business budget is particularly difficult when the entrepreneur has little or no knowledge of the probable costs associated with the business or the amount and timing of likely revenues. In many cases, owners forego budgeting while making operating and financial decisions in the hope that expenses will not exceed revenues.

Operating a home-based business without a budget is especially perilous due to the overlap between personal and business decisions. If, for example, the business operates at a loss and requires infusions of cash, the most likely source of investment is the business owner. In such cases, the owner might be forced to curtail or postpone important personal expenses to have the cash to pay the business expenses. Having a budget is no guarantee of business profitability, but its use can alert owners of potential business needs for future funds.

## THE IMPORTANCE OF VALID INFORMATION

Using guesses or averages without understanding one's personal spending habits usually ends with wide discrepancies between budgeted and actual expenses, making the budget practically worthless. People who work with computers understand the adage "Trash in, Trash out." In plain language, if you input wrong information, the output will also be wrong. If you create a budget with bad information, any comparison between the budget and your actual spending is likely to be misleading.

## COLLECTING FINANCIAL INFORMATION

The first task in preparing for a household or business budget is collecting and sorting your historical expenses to get a true picture of your financial situation. Whether you are creating a household or business budget, taking the time to review past expenditures is essential.

A careful review of your bank, credit card, and investment accounts will reveal the various sources and uses of your income. A copy of your latest income tax filing is also useful, especially if you want a total picture. At a minimum, you should collect three months of financial records (bank and credit card statements). Extend the review period if your expenses vary significantly during the year. For example, replacing or repairing a major appliance (refrigerator, air conditioner) or an automobile might happen at any time.

The effort required to collect information on past expenditures depends on its source and the details provided for each expenditure. If you are tempted to take shortcuts in collecting information, remember your original purpose in budgeting—to control your financial expenditures.

**Bank accounts**

Most people have one or more bank accounts that are used to deposit their cash income from different sources—salary, wages, gifts, etc.—and pay bills by electronic transfers, paper checks, automatic drafts, or a combination of all three. Collect all bank statements for the previous twelve months unless your bank prepares a summary of each account in a single document.

Figure 2 on the following page is an example of bank payments from three sources—paper checks, ATM withdrawals, and electronic payments. A review of each paper check is often necessary to determine the payee and use of the funds.

ATM withdrawals go into a catch-all category labeled "Cash." Unless you have maintained separate records for cash expenditures (which we recommend for Businesses in a Petty Cash account), the use of currency is, at best, an estimate. If you use cash regularly to avoid credit card interest or control your spending, consider using a "debit card" so payments are deducted from the account in real time and you have a record of the expense (payee name, date, and amount).

> ***WARNING: Using cash to pay bills or purchase items has some benefit if the amounts spent each month are less than 3% of your total income or you keep a physical record of each payment (a receipt, for example). Using cash for a significant amount of your expenditures is a drastic method of budgeting (when you are out of cash, you cannot spend more) and should only be in place until you can exercise more self-control.***

Figure 2 Sample Bank Statement

**CHECKS PAID**

| CHECK NO. | DESCRIPTION | DATE PAID | AMOUNT |
|---|---|---|---|
| 101 ^ | 03/12 | 03/12 | $145.00 |
| 103 * ^ | 03/31 | 03/31 | 30.00 |
| **Total Checks Paid** | | | **$175.00** |

If you see a description in the Checks Paid section, it means that we received only electronic information about the check, not the original or an image of the check. As a result, we're not able to return the check to you or show you an image.

* All of your recent checks may not be on this statement, either because they haven't cleared yet or they were listed on one of your previous statements.

^ An image of this check may be available for you to view on Chase.com.

**ATM & DEBIT CARD WITHDRAWALS**

| DATE | DESCRIPTION | AMOUNT |
|---|---|---|
| 03/09 | Card Purchase 03/07 [redacted] | $10.00 |
| 03/17 | Recurring Card Purchase 03/16 [redacted] | 143.86 |
| **Total ATM & Debit Card Withdrawals** | | **$153.86** |

**ELECTRONIC WITHDRAWALS**

| DATE | DESCRIPTION | AMOUNT |
|---|---|---|
| 03/09 | 03/09 Online Payment [redacted] | $113.68 |
| 03/09 | 03/09 Online Payment [redacted] | 23.00 |
| 03/09 | Farmers Ins [redacted] | 470.20 |
| 03/09 | Paypal Inst Xfer [redacted] | 198.38 |
| 03/18 | The Dallas Morni [redacted] | 63.65 |
| 03/19 | 03/19 Online Payment [redacted] | 600.00 |
| 03/19 | 03/19 Online Payment [redacted] | 600.00 |
| 03/19 | 03/19 Online Payment [redacted] | 500.00 |
| 03/20 | Best Egg Payment [redacted] | 94.86 |
| 03/23 | 03/23 Online Payment [redacted] AT&T U-Verse | 227.75 |
| 03/23 | 03/23 Online Payment [redacted] | 21.61 |
| 03/23 | Best Egg Payment [redacted] | 150.57 |
| 03/24 | 03/24 Online Payment [redacted] | 168.86 |
| 03/25 | 03/25 Online Payment [redacted] | 346.97 |

## Credit cards

Many finance companies prepare downloadable year-end summaries for account holders, often classified in specific expense categories. If you have copies of the year-end report, use them in place of monthly reports.

*TIP: Many banks and financial institutions allow customers who use electronic banking apps to assign categories (housing, food, auto, etc.) to each payee when setting up the payee account. Using this option will save you considerable time when reviewing expenses for budget or tax purposes.*

**Investment Accounts**

Collect the monthly statements from your investment and savings accounts, especially if you regularly contribute or withdraw funds from the accounts. The income from any investments, retirement or otherwise, that is consistent each month should be included as such. If you receive a one-time, lump-sum payment during a given month, then include it in that month only, and increase the appropriate expense category to reduce the net income to zero. An example of a one-time, lump-sum payment might be a settlement payout or an inheritance. Payments like this should follow this route for spending: pay off all debt, increase your emergency fund up to 6 months of expenses, ensure your retirement and college tuition accounts are appropriately funded, pay off the home mortgage, then live and give as you please.

# CHAPTER 5.
# CATEGORIZE INCOME & EXPENSES

Sorting the data into categories is essential to have information that you can use. Imagine trying to find a telephone number if the names of phone owners were in random order rather than alphabetized. The number of categories should be as few as possible to accurately reflect your general spending habits. You can slice and dice your income and expenses to the nth degree if you desire; however, this will only result in frustration and a drawn-out budgeting process for most people.

Our recommendation is to start with the example provided in the appendix labeled Personal Expense Categories and Home-Based Business Chart of Accounts. I do not recommend multiple subcategories for each main category, such as Insurance. All insurance payments go under the insurance category. All utilities for the home or business are included under the Utilities category. If I purchase any products or tools for home repair, then these expenses simply go under Repair.

*TIP: The effort and time required to sort and record expenses is directly proportional to the number of categories (or "accounts" in accounting jargon). Use the minimum number of categories that provide actionable information without generating trivia. For example, most budgeters are comfortable with the single category "Utilities" rather than setting up additional sub-categories like "electricity," "natural gas," "water," etc. Similarly, if you have one significant revenue source—your employment—you may not need additional sub-categories.*

## A WORD ABOUT NEEDS VERSUS WANTS

Every individual and business should categorize the essential expenses before any other expense that is considered a want. The essential expenses of the home budget consist of the four walls—the house payment, water and electricity, food, and required transportation. Once these are taken into account, the list moves onto secondary essentials and wants. Most people consider a means of communication—a telephone, for example—essential in our modern world, while a subscription to the HBO movie channel is considered a want. Similarly, owning an automobile for basic transportation might be necessary, but the decision to drive an expensive Mercedes versus a Chevrolet is a wish or a want. Learning to differentiate between needs and wants is crucial to living within one's means.

## SORTING INCOME AND EXPENSES INTO CATEGORIES

After determining your categories (you can change them if necessary), the next task is collecting your transactions into the proper categories. The process is the same for household and business budgets.

**Sorting the Income**

Begin with the first bank statement and highlight each deposit transaction with a specific color. Add up the total for the month, and repeat this step for at least 3 statements. Take the average income for the 3 months or the number of months you choose for historical accuracy. This will be the amount of monthly income that you use for each month's budget. In the case of a consistent amount deposited on a timely basis, you can use the expected deposit dates to calculate the income you will receive in a given month.

**Sorting the Expenses**

Next, using different colors for each category, highlight the expenses by their category. For example, all house payments will be highlighted green, and all utility payments might be red. Sum up the total of each category for each month, and then calculate the average expense total for the category across the number of months used. This is the average monthly expense total that you will use in your budget formula.

Some people use a spreadsheet with a header line of defined cells for each category (Figure 3). After reviewing each expense, transfer the dollar cost into the proper vertical category. When setting up the spreadsheet, consider using banded lines to separate categories for easier recognition of the correct entry cell.

*TIP: Using a variety of color markers (each category being a distinct color) to easily identify each expense visually will minimize input errors. When creating your spreadsheet, use the same colors to identify the vertical expense columns. See Figure 3 for example.*

Figure 3. Spreadsheet Sorting Example

| Expenses (April 1 -October 1, 2020) | | | | | | |
|---|---|---|---|---|---|---|
| Rent/Mtg | Utilities | Groceries | Auto | Entertainment | Medical | Insurance |
| 2,400 | 420 | 1,200 | 350 | 250 | 520 | 750 |
| 2,400 | 350 | 985 | 280 | 100 | 60 | 750 |
| 2,400 | 325 | 1,105 | 1,456 | 675 | 60 | 750 |
| 2,400 | 287 | 1,327 | 325 | 365 | 95 | 750 |
| 2,400 | 220 | 1,258 | 310 | 290 | 60 | 750 |
| 2,400 | 188 | 1,059 | 342 | 354 | 60 | 750 |

## WORKING WITH A HOUSEHOLD BUDGET

### Household Income Categories and Sub-categories

A typical household budget has a single catch-all category ("Income") to reflect the cash flows into the family, generally because the bulk of income is employee salaries and relatively stable. Some households track the incomes of each person in the household separately. The choice to do so is up to you.

Home business owners might elect to add a second income category ("Home-based Business Income) for budget purposes, since business profits that might be available to an owner are typically less certain than salary payments. Other income categories could be "Investment," "Retirement Plan," or "Gifts."

> *TIP: Remember, the purpose of a budget is to help manage your money so that you can pay all bills when they are due. Only use additional income categories if they will help you understand the in-and out flows of money from your account.*

> *→ WARNING: I caution the use of home-based business income for a start-up company. Many times, the take-home pay from such a business is small and inconsistent. Relying on such income to create a zero-based budget can create many headaches if your estimates are incorrect. If your business has been profitable for six or more months, use the average income for the period, "total income/# of months."*

## Household Expense Categories

First, recall that we always take care of the four walls first. These are essential household expenses that must be considered a priority and taken care of immediately. We will then consider the secondary essential household expenses and the wants (or discretionary expenses).

### *ESSENTIAL HOUSEHOLD EXPENSES*

Expenses that are essential to maintaining life will always go first. These four categories will likely change and grow with the size of your family;

however, all individuals need the following: shelter, food, water and electricity, and transportation. We will set these categories up first and calculate their monthly averages from our bank and credit card statement data.

The house payment should be a fixed amount each month. Water and Electricity, or Utilities, slightly vary in monthly cost, and their monthly averages should be used for budgeting purposes. The Food category only pertains to groceries and not any form of eating out. This amount should be fixed for each month and not vary by more than a few dollars. Transportation will vary depending on your work schedule and type; however, most families should be able to calculate an appropriate fuel and maintenance cost for each month.

From here, we must prioritize the remaining categories based on the level of need versus want. Home, health, and automotive insurance are needs, whereas any form of TV subscription is a want. Basic telecommunications is a need, but the latest iPhone with unlimited data is a want. As you complete your budget and find the leftover income, you can increase such categories to include the upgrades.

*TIP: Do not forget to consider Essential Household Expenses that occur less frequently than monthly. Many home mortgages may not include the cost of property taxes and insurance as an "escrow" item each month; however, they will be due at least once a year. Also, saving a few dollars each month for a semi-annual automotive expense such as an oil change is a good idea to ensure the cash is available when needed.*

### *DISCRETIONARY HOUSEHOLD EXPENSES*

Expenses which vary in amount each period usually depend on the decisions of the spender. Though some discretionary expenses might be considered necessities, include them in the discretionary category if they can be postponed for a time or easily reduced in amount. For example, expenditures for minor automobile repairs, painting the house, or dining out can be usually delayed in a pinch.

The decision about whether an expense is essential or discretionary is different for each person, so do not be afraid to rely on your judgment. Only you can decide whether your weekly donation to a charity is essential or discretionary.

> *TIP: Some expenses have Essential and Variable elements, such as the telephone & Internet expense. Some consider the fastest Internet service possible and a menu of premium movies and sports channels essential to mental health and would classify the expense as "Essential." Others who are willing to forego all premium telephone and Internet use might classify the expense as "Discretionary." Some split the expense between the two types. The decision of whether an expense is essential (required for life) or discretionary is personal and varies from one household to the next.*

## *A SAMPLE OF HOUSEHOLD EXPENSE CATEGORIES*

The following table lists expense categories found most often in household budgets. The list is neither mandatory nor exclusive, so select those that best fit your situation:

| | | |
|---|---|---|
| Rent/ Mortgage Payment | Clothing | Tax Liability |
| Utilities | Entertainment | Personal Care |
| Transportation | Automobile Expense | Insurance |
| Groceries | Travel & Vacation | Retirement & Investments |
| Medical & Dental | Phone | Debt Payments |
| Emergency Fund | Household Repairs | Cash & Miscellaneous |

*This list is not exhaustive and is only meant to provide examples.*

Many of the categories can be sub-divided where desired. For example, "Insurance" could be replaced with the sub-categories "Home Insurance," "Health Insurance," "Life Insurance," "Automobile Insurance," etc. When using sub-categories, be sure to isolate an expense to one category to avoid duplicate entries and the appearance of excessive expense. Automobile insurance might be included in "Automobile Expense" or "Insurance Expense," but not both.

## WORKING WITH A HOME-BASED BUSINESS BUDGET

The method used for sorting household expenses can be applied to a business budget if you have sufficient historical income and cost information to make reasonable estimates. Simply print out 12 months' worth of statements and begin your sorting process. When the information does not exist, you need to estimate your costs in each category using other sources:

- **Friends in the business**. A friend who owns a similar business and will not be a competitor can provide estimates based on their experience. In some cases, they might introduce you to a trusted supplier with invaluable insight about the future business.
- **Trade Associations**. Many businesses have trade groups or associations, which are collections of businesspeople in the same industry that associate formally and informally through social meetings, educational classes, and trade shows. In some instances, membership enables discounted prices on administrative products and services including insurance, retirement plans, human resources assistance, and financial preparations.
- **Suppliers**. The companies that provide materials and services have a vested interest in your success. They can be sources of valuable competitor information and potential buyers.
- **Professional advisers**. Accountants typically have experience and resources to help entrepreneurs get started. Lawyers and bankers are in the same group but may be less willing to share what they consider "confidential information."
- **Government agencies.** The Federal and various state governments have agencies that generate volumes of information about most small businesses. Potential sources include SCORE, the Small Business Administration, Small Business Development Centers, and Federal Business Opportunities (a database of

potential government contracts, many limited to small businesses only).

- **Small Business Associations.** The National Association for the Self-Employed and the National Federation of Independent Businesses may be able to help you with information and contacts.

There are magazines, newsletters, and websites dedicated to home-based businesses. One of the keys to small business success is to adopt a continuous learning mode. The more you know about your business, the more likely you will succeed.

### Business Income Categories

For a start-up company such as an online retailer, the single category "Income" is sufficient for budgeting. If you have two separate lines or products of business that differ from each other and have unique direct costs, using two income categories—one for each product, such as Product A Income, Service B Income—might be warranted. When using more than the single category "Income," you should consider identifying the direct costs for each in your budget expenses. This is an advanced budgeting method and is NOT required to provide an accurate net income at the end of the month. We will attempt to introduce this method here.

### Business Expense Categories and Sub-Categories

Expenditures in a business differ from those in a household budget, being classified as either "fixed" or "variable." Variable expenses apply to direct costs that fluctuate with volume, and they represent the direct cost of your inventory or services provided to a client. For our purposes, we will label the Variable Business Expenses as Cost of Goods Sold on our simplified budget and all other costs as Fixed Business Expenses.

*Figure 5.1 Sample Format Business Budget*

| BUSINESS BUDGET FORMAT | |
|---|---|
| **Revenues** | |
| Product A | |
| Product B | |
| ***Total Revenues*** | |
| **Expenses** | |
| Cost Of Goods Sold | |
| Product A | |
| Product B | |
| ***Total Cost of Goods Sold*** | |
| Fixed Costs | |
| Fixed Cost 1 | |
| Fixed Cost 2 | |
| ***Total Fixed Costs*** | |
| **Total Expenses** | |
| **Net Income (Loss)** | |

## *VARIABLE BUSINESS EXPENSES*

For a retail business, the Cost of Goods Sold (COGS), or variable expenses, are displayed first in a business budget because they are a required cost to obtain the product or service that you are going to sell. You could also consider these costs essential to your business. COGS change in proportion to operations and sales levels each month. They rise as activity increases and fall when activity declines. For example, if you sell jewelry, then the wholesale price of a necklace to your business is COGS. If you sell more necklaces this month than last month, then your Variable Costs will increase due to an increase in the cost of that particular inventory item.

Examples of business variable expense categories include the purchase or production of a product or service and the labor involved, packaging, shipping in and out, and materials purchased. As a rule, any expense that varies in parallel with revenue growth is a variable expense. Consider these costs as essential to the business because they directly affect how much revenue you can produce in a given month.

For a service-based business, COGS can be ignored, and the budget becomes simplified. All expenses can be considered "Fixed" and will be netted against a single income category. For an in-depth discussion concerning advanced budgeting and reporting techniques for businesses, we recommend that you visit our website at www.barkleeinstitute.com.

## *FIXED BUSINESS EXPENSES*

Sometimes referred to as overhead or indirect costs, fixed costs are the ongoing business expenses that do not vary in amount from one period to the next. Examples include rent, equipment leasing, insurance, and administrative payroll costs that continue regardless of the business's operating levels or income.

The indirect expense categories for home-based businesses are usually similar across industries, so there is no particular need to create new ones solely based on your business. Just as in the household budget, the more categories that you add to the list, the more confusing and complex the budget will become. You can find an example budget for product and service-based businesses in the appendix. Also, we provide a list of examples for business categories here for quick reference.

**Examples of indirect, or fixed, expense categories for home-based businesses**

| | | |
|---|---|---|
| Owner Salaries | Automobile Expenses | Advertising |
| Insurance | Legal/ Professional Fees | Office Supplies/ Administration Expense |
| Subscriptions & Dues | Cost of Goods Sold | Education/ Training |
| Licenses | Interest Expense / Payment Center Fees | Business Equipment |
| Lease/ Rental Fees | Wages or Contractor Fees | Debt Payments |

Home-based business expenses should be separated from household expenses for tax and management purposes, although the distinction between the two can be confusing. After collecting, categorizing, collating, and summarizing your data, your next step is an analysis of the data and assigning values for your budget.

*Warning: Home-based businesses that operate out of a home do not typically pay rent or utilities. These expenses are paid for from the household budget, and your tax preparer will properly account for them on your tax return. The IRS has detailed instructions for the filing of a home office deduction (IRS Form 8829) with the amount reported on Schedule C of the Form 1040.*

# CHAPTER 6.
# FORMAT A HOUSEHOLD BUDGET

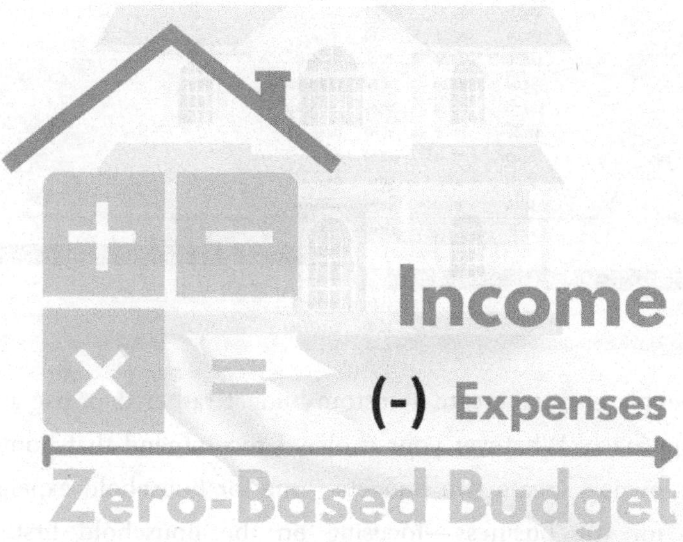


The formula for a budget is as follows: With the single exception of separating income from expenses, the visual format of a budget is not fixed. There are a variety of downloadable household and budget worksheet templates available for a nominal cost or free on the Internet or included in Microsoft Excel. Most are easily customized to fit specific circumstances. Figure 6.1 illustrates a popular Excel Household Budget template.

Figure 6.1 Downloadable Excel Household Budget Template

## Personal Monthly Budget

| Projected Monthly Income | |
|---|---|
| Income 1 | $4,300.00 |
| Extra income | $300.00 |
| Total monthly income | $4,600.00 |

| Actual Monthly Income | |
|---|---|
| Income 1 | $4,000.00 |
| Extra income | $300.00 |
| Total monthly income | $4,300.00 |

| | |
|---|---|
| Projected Balance (Projected income minus expenses) | $3,405.00 |
| Actual Balance (Actual income minus expenses) | $3,064.00 |
| Difference (Actual minus projected) | ($341.00) |

| HOUSING | Projected Cost | Actual Cost | Difference |
|---|---|---|---|
| Mortgage or rent | $1,000.00 | $1,000.00 | $0.00 |
| Phone | $54.00 | $100.00 | -$46.00 |
| Electricity | $44.00 | $56.00 | -$12.00 |
| Gas | $22.00 | $28.00 | -$6.00 |
| Water and sewer | $8.00 | $8.00 | $0.00 |
| Cable | $34.00 | $34.00 | $0.00 |
| Waste removal | $10.00 | $10.00 | $0.00 |
| Maintenance or repairs | $23.00 | $0.00 | $23.00 |
| Supplies | $0.00 | $0.00 | $0.00 |
| Other | $0.00 | $0.00 | $0.00 |
| Subtotal | | | -$41.00 |

| TRANSPORTATION | Projected Cost | Actual Cost | Difference |
|---|---|---|---|
| Vehicle payment | | | $0.00 |
| Bus/taxi fare | | | $0.00 |

| ENTERTAINMENT | Projected Cost | Actual Cost | Difference |
|---|---|---|---|
| Video/DVD | | | $0.00 |
| CDs | | | $0.00 |
| Movies | | | $0.00 |
| Concerts | | | $0.00 |
| Sporting events | | | $0.00 |
| Live theater | | | $0.00 |
| Other | | | $0.00 |
| Other | | | $0.00 |
| Other | | | $0.00 |
| Subtotal | | | $0.00 |

| LOANS | Projected Cost | Actual Cost | Difference |
|---|---|---|---|
| Personal | | | $0.00 |
| Student | | | $0.00 |
| Credit card | | | $0.00 |

Many people elect to create a custom budget rather than use a cookie-cutter approach. Whatever your choice, I recommend that home-based business owners create two budgets—one for household expenses and another for the business—focusing on the household first. As an entrepreneur myself, I realize that the household budget may not be able to claim a consistent business income from the initial start-up. Also, the owners of many new businesses may be required to add funds to the business in an emergency. Having a valid household budget enables business owners to know if and how much funds might be available to transfer to the business.

## CREATING A CUSTOMIZED HOME BUDGET

I have always developed custom budgets rather than using a template for maximum flexibility. Use the following steps to quickly create your custom home budget in Excel.

**1. Set up the basic form.**

After entering the name of the form in the merged cells (A1:D2) across the top, label the first four columns on Row 3 as Income/Expense, Sub-category, Total-Category, and Budget. Note this spreadsheet is for the Household Budget.

| | A | B | C | D |
|---|---|---|---|---|
| 1–2 | **John and Jane Doe Monthly Household Budget** | | | |
| 3 | **Income/Expense** | **Sub-Category** | **Total-Category** | **Budget** |

Title cell A4 "Income" to identify the group of entries as income-related. Note that I have recognized the possibility of multiple income sources. If you have just one source, enter the amount in Cell B4, leaving cells B5:B8 blank. If you have multiple sources of income, label them in column A under "Income" in cell A4. In the example, I have accounted for two separate incomes—the income from the home business (I will deal with that later) and "Other" to capture any other income that the household receives.

Note that the Total Income from all sources appears in cell C9. This use of sub-categories and categories is useful. Also, if you want to see just a Total, you can "hide" rows 5 through 8.

| | A | B | | C | | D |
|---|---|---|---|---|---|---|
| 1 | John and Jane Doe Monthly Household Budget | | | | | |
| 2 | | | | | | |
| 3 | Income/ Expense | Sub-Category | | Total Category | | Budget |
| 4 | Income | | | | | |
| 5 | Income #1 | $ | 8,750 | | | |
| 6 | Income #2 | $ | 6,340 | | | |
| 7 | Home Business | | | | | |
| 8 | Other | $ | 560 | | | |
| 9 | Total Income | | | $ | 15,650 | |
| 10 | | | | | | |

Consider the following example of the fictitious Doe family, the co-owners of Jane's Custom Sundresses, to illustrate the process. The Doe couple decided to start a new business when Jane's employer relocated to the West Coast. Fortunately, she negotiated a severance agreement with her former employer to continue her salary and healthcare benefits for six months. Her husband, John, continues his work as a partner in a medium-sized law firm. In addition to their salaries, the couple receives an annual dividend from John's father's estate.

John receives a $15,000 monthly salary from the firm with a net pay of $10,000 after taxes and deductions. He also receives a distribution of his firm's annual profits of $65,000 after taxes and annualizes for budget purposes. Jane's severance pay after deductions is $5,333 but will end after six months. The couple also receives $1,150 monthly from John's father's estate.

## 2. Calculate Income

The first step in the budgeting process is to identify the ongoing income that is expected. After opening a new Excel spreadsheet, input the titles "Sources of Income," "Amount," and "Total" in adjacent horizontal cells on the spreadsheet. You can add color to the cell or text to highlight specific cells. Enter the information on the couple's income per example. Note that the distribution of the law firm's profits is not included as income in the budget, and I have added a note that Jane's income is limited to six months.

| The Does' Household Budget | | |
|---|---|---|
| **Sources of Income** | **Amount** | **Total** |
| John's Net Pay | $ 10,000 | |
| Jane's Net Pay* | $ 5,333 | |
| John's Inheritance | $ 1,150 | |
| **Total Sources** | | $ 16,483 |
| * Ends in six months | | |

*WARNING: Including an annual bonus in your household budget can lead to overspending and budget deficits. Bonuses are not typically guaranteed. A rule of thumb to follow in budgeting and money management is do not spend until you have the funds on hand. Rather than include a prorated amount in your monthly budget, use the bonus to pay off debt or retain it as an emergency fund.*

*TIP: Consider having contributions to your retirement accounts deducted from your gross pay just as taxes and employer-sponsored healthcare premiums are deducted. This method ensures that retirement savings are made each month automatically.*

### 3. Calculate a Monthly Household Expense

To determine your historical average expense for a specific category, add the individual expenditures in each category, then divide the total by the number of months considered in the data (total expense/number of months of data). For example, if the total spent on groceries for six months is $6,934, the average per month is $1,156. Do the calculation for each expense category and transfer the result to your budget model (Figure 6.2).

*Figure 6.2 Calculating Budget Expense*

Expenses (April 1-October 1, 2020)

| | Rent/Mtg | Utilities | Groceries | Auto | Entertainment | Medical |
|---|---|---|---|---|---|---|
| | 2400 | 420 | 1200 | 350 | 250 | [illegible] |
| | 2400 | 350 | 985 | 280 | 100 | |
| | 2400 | 325 | 1105 | 1456 | 675 | |
| | 2400 | 287 | 1327 | 325 | [illegible] | |
| | 2400 | 220 | 1258 | 310 | | |
| | 2400 | 188 | 1059 | 342 | | |
| Total 6 mos | $ 14,400 | $ 1,790 | $ 6,934 | $ [illegible] | | |
| AVG month | $ 2,400 | $ 298 | $ 1,156 | $ | | |

Before entering your averages in your budget, consider each category of expenses for changes that are likely to occur. For example, utilities and insurance premiums frequently change, so you want to be sure you have enough allocated for those costs and others like them. Similarly, you may want to reduce some figures to cut discretionary expenses such as TV cable packages, subscriptions, or dining out.

Your goal at a minimum is to have sufficient income to cover your budgeted expenses. If you have a deficit, you will need to either increase revenues or cut expenses.

### 4. Enter your Data into the Household Budget

The last step in preparing your budget is entering the data into the budget spreadsheet. Check your calculations to be sure the entries are correct. Some budget users keep a running total of their expenses as the month goes by to check their progress. Doing so might save you time at the end of the month, but the effort can be inconvenient.

*TIP: Review your budget physically once a week and before you make any large expenditures to keep its importance uppermost in your mind.*

# CHAPTER 7.
# FORMAT A HOME-BASED BUSINESS BUDGET

While the process for creating a household and home-based budget is similar, there are notable differences:

- **Income sources.** Only revenues that are directly attributed to the business should be included in the business. Salaries and bonuses from other employment, retirement funds, gifts, and inheritances belong in your household budget. Intermingling the sources creates complications, invalidates business analysis, and jeopardizes favorable income tax treatment.
- **Fixed expenses.** Most fixed expenses for a home-based business are the consequence of personal needs, i.e., they exist independently from a business. To the extent they affect business costs, they are reported separately on income tax forms. Include only those expenses directly attributable to the business, such as product liability insurance in the fixed expense category.
- **Variable expenses.** All expenses that are used for the production or delivery of a product or service that also fluctuate in value in response to the sales volume are indirect and reported in the Variable expense section of the budget.
- **Surpluses and Deficits.** Excess income over expense (Surplus) is income that can be (1) distributed to the owners as personal income or (2) retained in the business as an asset. Surplus income

adds to owner equity. Excess expense over income produces a negative result (Deficit) that is offset by infusions of capital or a reduction in owner equity.

## ENTER DATA IN BUDGET TEMPLATE

The last step in preparing your home-based business budget is transferring your estimates of future income and expenses to the budget spreadsheet. Check your calculations to be sure the entries are correctly transposed.

Review your bottom line. In most cases, you should strive for sufficient revenues to produce a break-even. Before settling on the final budget numbers, review each estimate and validate its underlying assumptions.

## CALCULATING BREAK-EVEN REVENUES

Each home-based business owner should know the sales volume necessary to break-even—the point where all expenses can be paid without any surplus. The break-even point in units sold (***BE***) is calculated by dividing the fixed costs of the business (***FC***) by the difference in the price charged per unit (***P***) minus the variable costs of providing each unit (***VC***).

$$BE = FC/(P - VC)$$

Example: The hypothetical Does' family business—Jane's Custom Sundresses—has direct costs for material, labor, and shipping of $50 a dress. Also, they have fixed costs of $2200 per month for a website and marketing program. They intend to sell each dress for $90 including free shipping. To break-even, they must sell 55 dresses each month.

$$BE = \$2200/(\$90 - \$50)$$

$$BE = \ 55\ units$$

A break-even calculation is an important tool for home-based business owners because it illustrates the relationships between its three determinants. Consider the effects of changes in the three factors—price, variable costs, and fixed costs—on break-even:

- **Increasing the price of the sales unit**. Since direct costs remain unchanged, a higher price produces more cash to pay fixed costs, reduce a deficit, or produce a profit. A business owner should strive for the highest price possible unless its level gives competitors an advantage or deters customer purchases. Lowering the sales price will increase the number of units sold necessary to break-even. Before lowering the price of a product, an owner should consider whether the lower cost will attract sufficient new sales to recover the smaller difference between price and variable costs.
- **Decreasing the variable costs of the sales unit.** In our example, the variable costs per unit were $50. To lower costs, the owners might find a less expensive cloth supplier, use a lower cost material, or reduce the labor costs by speeding up production. If the sales price of $90 remains stable, there will be more cash to pay fixed costs. Before implementing measures to reduce variable costs, owners should consider their effect on the quality of their product or potential labor problems arising from an increase in production.
- **Decreasing the fixed costs of the organization**. Reducing fixed costs reduces the number of units sold necessary to break-even, like a reduction in variable costs. Exchanging fixed costs for variable costs for most home-based businesses is a good strategy since variable costs are controllable. For example, many small businesses rely on contract labor rather than employees, even though the former might cost more per hour due to the ability to match the labor force with sales demand.

Table 7.1 illustrates the relationships of Break-Even influences.

Figure 7.1 Break-Even Table

| Fixed Costs | Price less Variable Cost Per Unit | | | | |
|---|---|---|---|---|---|
| | $ 25 | $ 30 | $ 35 | $ 40 | $ 50 |
| $2,700 | 108 | 90 | 77 | 68 | 54 |
| $2,600 | 104 | 87 | 74 | 65 | 52 |
| $2,500 | 100 | 83 | 71 | 63 | 50 |
| $2,400 | 96 | 80 | 69 | 60 | 48 |
| $2,300 | 92 | 77 | 66 | 58 | 46 |
| $2,200 | 88 | 73 | 63 | 55 | 44 |
| $2,000 | 80 | 67 | 57 | 50 | 40 |

## REVIEW THE BUDGET AND ADJUST AS NECESSARY

Before settling on your business budget estimates, review the results and consider the following:

1. Will I break-even if I meet my budget numbers? Do I have the resources to cover any expected deficits?
2. Are my sales estimates reasonable? Could the price be higher without hurting the expected sales volume? Can I charge separately for costs like packaging and shipping?
3. Are my variable costs realistic or optimistic? Is there any way I could lower the direct costs of producing my sales such as different suppliers, materials, packaging, or labor costs?
4. Have I included each of my fixed costs? Can I reduce my fixed costs by renegotiation or elimination? Can I substitute variable costs for any fixed costs?

Make any appropriate adjustments in your estimates that you are confident can be achieved. Your goal at a minimum is to have sufficient income to cover your budgeted expenses. If you have a deficit, you will need to either increase revenues or cut expenses. However, you do not want to fool yourself. Your budget is a valuable tool if the information is valid. As a practical matter, the actual results should be within five percent (5%) of your estimates, barring a major surprise.

# CHAPTER 8.
# THE BENEFIT OF CONSERVATIVE ESTIMATES

A general rule of forecasting—in this case, estimating the dollar amounts of income and expenses—is to err on the conservative side.

- **Estimating monthly sales**. If you have no idea of your future sales, then use "0" as income. The effect of no sales will produce a negative cash balance at the end of the budget period equal to the total costs for the period, an amount that must be added to the company to stay in business. That is the worst possible outcome and highly unlikely if you have a good business idea. As time goes by, you will have a better feel for future sales and can adjust your budget numbers.
- **Estimating monthly expenses.** When estimating revenues, it is better to go low—forecasting fewer sales—than high. Conversely, when estimating expenses for your budget, it is better to be high than low. In other words, projecting higher costs than what might appear ensures you will not experience a surprise when the actual results are calculated. You might be pleasantly surprised.

## JANE'S CUSTOM SUNDRESSES

To emphasize the value of conservative estimates, consider the hypothetical home-based business co-owned by John and Jane Doe that makes and sells custom sundresses. Since my purpose is to show the different impacts of conservative and aggressive estimates, I have simplified the budget by eliminating indirect expense items and exaggerating the revenue expectations to better illustrate the outcomes. My assumptions include the use of cash rather than an accrual, which is an accounting system, and I have disregarded any increase in inventory.

The couple has agreed to produce 80 dresses each month until demand requires a greater volume. They know that material for each dress costs $15 and about two hours of labor at $15 per hour or $45 total cost. Pricing each dress with a 100% markup sets a market price of $90 per dress, slightly below the prices of similar dresses offered by the local competitors.

### Jane's Estimate

Being the more conservative of the two partners, Jane is uncomfortable projecting any level of sales until the business has some history. Also, she believes that the production time for each dress is likely to take two and a half hours instead of two, the early estimate, raising her estimate of labor expense for each dress from $30 to $37.50. Her total dress cost is $52.50. Jane's projected budget indicates that the business will have a loss of $4,200 in the first month. An outsider might question why anyone would invest in a small business that would not produce any sales in a month of operations.

## John's Estimate

John, being an eternal optimist, is sure that the dresses will fly off the shelves as soon as they are produced. His estimate includes selling all eighty dresses at the $90 price. He also believes that the seamstresses will be faster than expected due to experience. He anticipates that labor hours to sew each dress will be one hour and forty-five minutes for a labor expense of $26.25 per dress and a total dress cost of $41.25. John's projected budget assumes a profit of $3,900 this first month. In financial circles, John's optimism is known as "eating the cake before it's out of the oven."

| | John & Jane Custom Sun Dresses | | | |
|---|---|---|---|---|
| | Jane-Conservative | | John-Aggressive | |
| | Budget | Actual | Budget | Actual |
| Sales ($90 per dress) | 0 | 25 | 80 | 25 |
| Income | $ - | $ 2,250 | $ 7,200 | $ 2,250 |
| less Expenses | $ 4,200 | $ 3,600 | $ 3,300 | $ 3,600 |
| Gross Profit | $ (4,200) | $ (1,350) | $ 3,900 | $ (1,350) |
| Impact | | $ (2,850) | | $ 5,250 |

## Actual Results Versus Estimates

When the month ended for our fictional company, twenty-five dresses had been sold—well above Jane's estimate and well below John's optimistic expectations. Had the couple agreed on Jane's estimate, they would have received a pleasant surprise, expecting to lose $4,200 for the month. On the other hand, if they had settled on John's estimate, a loss of $1350 when they expected a gain of $3,900 would be devastating.

## Conclusions

Both budgets are off the mark to the extent that they are unusable for planning or performance measurement. Here's why:

- Jane's pessimistic estimate of sales volume required keeping extra cash available that might have been better utilized in marketing cost or producing more dresses for sale.
- John's budget was so far over the top that cash needed to pay expenses might have been spent on other items or distributed as income to the two partners requiring an unexpected effort to find money to pay bills.

# CHAPTER 9.
# COMPARE BUDGET TO ACTUALS

Before we begin this chapter, I want to explain a personal belief of mine that has led to our financial peace. The household budget should rarely deviate from the actual spending during a month. If a surprise expense arises, then you should go to the budget immediately and decide what other expense categories you are going to reduce to maintain a zero-based budget.

A business budget, however, can drastically change if sales skyrocket for a given month. Greater variability is often found in the home-based business budget for this reason, and this is where the analysis for adjustments should take place.

Creating a budget and never looking at it is akin to planning a vacation and leaving your plans at home. You might remember some details, but the likelihood of missing an important site on your trip is high. A budget is a fantastic tool when used often and correctly to keep your financial journey on track.

## ADAPTING SPREADSHEET FOR ANALYSIS

At the end of each budget period, you will need to set up your budget for analysis:

1. Calculate your actual spending with totals in each budget category, then transfer your results to the budget spreadsheet under a column named "**Actual**."
2. Create a third column titled "**$ Variation**" for the cash difference between your budget's estimated expenditures and your actual expenditure.
3. Set up a fourth column titled "**% Variation**" to calculate the percentage difference between your budget and your actual expenditures. Knowing the percentage difference is necessary to prioritize your analysis.
4. Launch a fifth column titled "**Revised Budget**" for the changes that you make in the budget following your analysis.

## ANALYZING ACTUALS VERSUS BUDGET

A comparison of budget estimates and actual expenditures identifies variations between the two values. In most cases, variations will exist simply because the future is not known, i.e., the reason for estimates. The key to subsequent analysis is knowing which variations are important and the causes of those variations. When I analyze a budget, I use the following questions to ensure I consider each possibility that may need adjustment:

❶ **Did I spend more than my income for the period?** A "Yes" answer means that I must cover the deficit by using savings or borrowing money, probably on a credit card. Spending more than you earn is a sure road to financial ruin and cannot be supported indefinitely.

2 **Which categories did I underestimate or overestimate by more than 5%?** Some variations are to be expected, so I do not worry about small variations. You can set your boundary, but any category of income or expense that is over the boundary warrants extra scrutiny.

3 **Is the dollar amount of the identified category significant?** In some cases, a high percentage is the consequence of the dollar amount of the category. For example, if I estimate $50 a month for automobile fuel and spend $75, the percentage variation is 50%. While the percentage variation draws my attention, the dollar amounts involved are insignificant. Conversely, a large dollar amount even if the percentage variation is below my boundary will attract my attention.

After identifying a meaningful variation, I consider its possible causes and the adjustments I might make to better manage my results. In some cases, the cause is a lack of discipline on my part; in others, outside factors such as higher vendor prices, illness, or an unexpected repair is the reason for the discrepancy.

## ADJUSTING BUDGET FOR FUTURE PERIODS

4 **Do I need to change my budget estimates for future months?** My analysis allows me to adjust my budget if necessary to better reflect future periods. With the new actual results, my estimate of future income and expenses should become more reliable. More reliable budgets mean fewer surprises and less need to take emergency actions.

Examples of a Household and Business Budget are Figures 9.1 and 9.2 on the following pages.

## Figure 9.1 Comparison of Household Budget versus Actual Expenditures

| HOUSEHOLD BUDGET vs Actuals | Budget Sept 2020 | Actual Sept 2020 | $ Variation | % Variation | Rev Budget Oct 2020 |
|---|---|---|---|---|---|
| **Income** | | | | | |
| Ptr 1 - Net Pay* | 3,500 | (3) 3,420 | -80 | (2) -2.29% | (4) 3,500 |
| Ptr 2 - Net Pay* | 1,800 | 1,925 | 125 | 6.94% | 1,800 |
| Interest Paid | | | | | |
| Inhertiances | | | | | |
| Gifts | 50 | 250 | 200 | 400% | |
| Other | | | | | |
| **Total Income** | $ 5,350 | $ 5,595 | $ 245 | 4.58% | $ 5,300 |
| **Expenses** | | | | | |
| Rent/Mtg Payment** | 850 | 850 | 0 | 0.00% | 850 |
| Util-Elec, Gas, Water | 125 | 245 | 120 | 96.00% | 265 |
| Digital - Net, TV, phone | 500 | 375 | -125 | -25.00% | 375 |
| Home Security | 55 | 55 | 0 | 0.00% | 55 |
| Food @ home | 850 | 650 | -200 | -23.53% | 750 |
| Clothing | 75 | 0 | -75 | -100.00% | 75 |
| Auto Payment | 320 | 320 | 0 | 0.00% | 320 |
| Fuel | 75 | 115 | 40 | 53.33% | 125 |
| Auto repair/maint. | 50 | 0 | -50 | -100.00% | 50 |
| Charities | 50 | 200 | 150 | 300.00% | 50 |
| Insurance -Property | 300 | 300 | 0 | 0.00% | 300 |
| Insurance - Life | 75 | 75 | 0 | 0.00% | 75 |
| Insurance - Health | 225 | 225 | 0 | 0.00% | 225 |
| Medical | 100 | 60 | -40 | -40.00% | 100 |
| Retirement (IRAs) | 500 | 500 | 0 | 0.00% | 500 |
| Entertainment | 150 | 420 | 270 | 180.00% | 250 |
| Travel/Vacations | 0 | 0 | 0 | | 0 |
| Credit Card Payments | 75 | 325 | 250 | 333.33% | 100 |
| Miscellaneous | 125 | 145 | 20 | 16.00% | 125 |
| **Total Expenses** | $ 4,500 | $ 4,860 | $ 360 | 8.00% | $ 4,590 |
| **Surplus (Deficit)** (1) | $ 850 | $ 735 | $ (115) | -13.53% | $ 710 |

* **After taxes and other deductions**
** **include pro rata share of property taxes**

## Figure 9.2 Comparison of Business Budget and Actual Expenditures

| MONTHLY BUSINESS BUDGET PROJECTIONS | Budget - Sept 2020 | Actual Sept 2020 | $ Variation | % Variation | Rev Budget Oct 2020 |
|---|---|---|---|---|---|
| Income | | | | | |
| Products | 25,000 | 29,000 | 4000 | 16.00% | 28,000 |
| **Total Income** | $ 25,000 | $ 29,000 | $ 4,000 | 16.00% | $ 28,000 |
| **Expenses (Variable)** | | | | | |
| Labor | 3,500 | 2,800 | -700 | -20.00% | 2,800 |
| Inventory | 16,250 | 18,850 | 2600 | 16.00% | 16,250 |
| Marketing (Adv, Mail, SEO) | 500 | 500 | 0 | 0.00% | 1,500 |
| Travel | 100 | 82 | -18 | -18.00% | 100 |
| Entertainment | 100 | 145 | 45 | 45.00% | 200 |
| Ofc Exps (Printing, mail, etc) | 100 | 100 | 0 | 0.00% | 100 |
| Legal/Prof fees | 25 | 25 | 0 | 0.00% | 25 |
| Sales Taxes | 2,000 | 2,320 | 320 | 16.00% | 2,240 |
| **Total Expenses (Variable)** | $ 20,550 | $ 22,477 | $ 1,927 | 9.38% | $ 20,950 |
| **Expenses (Fixed)** | | | | | |
| Employee/Contractor Expense** | 1,200 | 1,200 | - | 0.00% | 1,200 |
| Employee Taxes** | 92 | 92 | - | 0.00% | 92 |
| Rent** | - | - | - | 0.00% | - |
| Utilities** | - | - | - | 0.00% | - |
| Digital (Internet, phone) | 230 | 247 | 17 | 7.39% | 250 |
| Insurance - Liability | 100 | 100 | - | 0.00% | 100 |
| Taxes - Business | 2,000 | 2,320 | 320 | 16.00% | 2,240 |
| Loan Repayments | 600 | 600 | - | 0.00% | 600 |
| **Total Expenses (Fixed)** | $ 4,222 | $ 4,559 | $ 337 | 7.98% | $ 4,482 |
| **Total Expenses** | $ 24,772 | $ 27,036 | $ (2,264) | 9.14% | $ 25,432 |
| Surplus (Deficit) | $ 228 | $ 1,964 | | | $ 2,568 |
| **Cash flow from Personal** | $ 850 | $ 735 | $ (115) | $ (0) | $ 710 |
| **Cash flow from Business** | $ 228 | $ 1,964 | $ 1,736 | #REF! | #REF! |
| **Net Cash Flow monthly** | $ 1,078 | $ 2,699 | $ 1,621 | #REF! | #REF! |

# CHAPTER 10.
# MERGE HOUSEHOLD AND BUSINESS BUDGETS

While the budgets of a household and a home-based business should be separate for tax and strategic reasons, the link between the two is inescapable. At the end of the day, the result of the business can have a major impact on the finances of the household.

- When the business produces a cash flow deficit, the business owner may be forced to reduce household expenditures to pay business expenses.
- When the business produces a cash flow surplus, the household may have extra funds to spend or save.

Figure 10.1 illustrates a simple spreadsheet capture and displays the combined results of the two accounts with a column for projected results in the upcoming period of comparison.

Figure 10.1 Combined Results of Household and Business Incomes

| RECONCILIATION OF HOUSEHOLD & BUSINESS INCOMES | Budget Sept 2020 | Actual Sept 2020 | $ Variation | % Variation | Rev Budget Oct 2020 |
|---|---|---|---|---|---|
| **Household Income** | $ 850 | $ 735 | $ (115) | 13.53% | $ 710 |
| **Business Income** | $ 228 | $ 1,964 | $ 1,736 | 760.74% | $ 1,500 |
| **Total Income vs Plan** | $ 1,078 | $ 2,699 | $ 1,621 | 150.34% | $ 2,210 |

*WARNING: Do not include any income from your home-based business in your household budget unless the business has made consistent profits for a minimum of six months. If your business has been profitable for six or more months, use the average income for the period—(total income/# of months).*

# APPENDIX A

## A SIMPLE HOUSEHOLD BUDGET EXAMPLE WITH CATEGORIES

This example is intended to be a starter budget for any beginner. Simply reproduce this budget and fill in the transaction amounts for each month using the process outlined in this book. We highly recommend that you do not attempt to make new categories for single transactions; rather, find a category for each type of transaction to fit in. As you grow comfortable with your budget, you can add categories when appropriate.

## PERSONAL BUDGET - SIMPLE

(INCOME - EXPENSES = NET INCOME)

| | |
|---|---|
| **INCOME** | |
| Wages & Salaries | |
| Business Income | |
| Other | |
| **INCOME TOTAL** | |
| | |
| **EXPENSES** | |
| Mortgage or Rent Expense | |
| Groceries | |
| Utilities | |
| Fuel | |
| Property Taxes Fund | |
| Income & SE Taxes Fund | |
| Insurance | |
| Automotive Repairs & Maintenance | |
| Home Repairs | |
| Emergency Fund | |
| Retirement Investments | |
| Debt Payments | |
| Clothing | |
| Personal Care & Hygiene | |
| Donations | |
| Health and Medical Expenses | |
| Storage & Other Rent Expense | |
| Dues & Subscriptions | |
| Education | |
| Vacation Expenses | |
| Fun Money | |
| Holidays and Birthdays | |
| Restaurants | |
| Miscellaneous Expense | |
| **EXPENSES TOTAL** | |
| | |
| **NET INCOME** (ZERO-BASED BUDGET) | |

## A SIMPLE HOME-BASED BUSINESS BUDGET EXAMPLE WITH CATEGORIES

The home-based business budget needs to include categories that are specific to the business only. Reproduce this budget and add categories that might be specific to your business only as needed.

| Home-Based Business Budget (Gross Revenue - COGS - Expenses = How much I can pay myself) | | | |
|---|---|---|---|
| **Income** | | **Expenses** | |
| GROSS REVENUE (PRODUCT OR SERVICES) | | SALARIES AND WAGES | |
| OTHER INCOME | | EMPLOYEE BENEFITS | |
| **Total Income** | | PAYROLL TAX EXPENSES | |
| | | CONTRACT LABOR | |
| **Cost of Goods Sold** (IF APPLICABLE) | | RENT & LEASE | |
| COST OF PRODUCT | | DEBT PAYMENTS | |
| COST OF LABOR | | INTEREST, BANK, & PAYMENT FEES | |
| COST OF SERVICES | | PROPERTY TAX - BUSINESS | |
| COST OF FREIGHT | | INSURANCE - BUSINESS | |
| DISCOUNTS | | INSURANCE OTHER | |
| SALES TAX | | LICENSING & PERMITS | |
| TOTAL COGS | | STATE INCOME TAX | |
| **Gross Profit** | | OTHER TAXES | |
| | | LEGAL FEES | |
| | | ACCOUNTING & TAX PREPARATION | |
| | | SOFTWARE | |
| | | UTILITIES | |
| | | SUPPLIES | |
| | | OFFICE SUPPLIES | |
| | | POSTAGE | |
| | | FREIGHT | |
| | | ADVERTISING | |
| | | MEALS - BUSINESS | |
| | | DUES & SUBSCRIPTIONS | |
| | | TRAVEL | |
| | | AUTOMOTIVE EXPENSE | |
| | | FUEL | |
| | | REPAIRS | |
| | | PROFESSIONAL EDUCATION | |
| | | DONATIONS - BUSINESS | |
| | | MISCELLANEOUS EXPENSE | |
| | | **TOTAL EXPENSES** | |
| | | **NET INCOME** (a.k.a. Owners' Salary) | |

# ABOUT THE AUTHOR

**Jeremy Knight, DVM** is a double graduate of Oklahoma State University where he earned his doctorate in Veterinary Medicine and then began his education in accounting and finance. His experience as a surgical and critical care director for Texas' largest referral hospitals has provided him keen insight on cash flow management, business operations, accounting processes, employee management, and payroll, as well as business model development and implementation.

Dr. Knight furthered his accounting and financial education at Texas Tech University in Lubbock, Texas where his firm operates as a Virtual Chief Financial Officer and Investment Advisor for many small businesses and individuals. His current focus is primarily on small-business financial plans and tax strategies. Also, Dr. Knight pours his financial knowledge and practicality into his community as a Financial Peace University Coordinator.

Jeremy, and all his resources, can be found by visiting:

**www.thebarkleeinstitute.com**

Made in the USA
Monee, IL
05 November 2026

67375681R00042